A Note to Parents a

DK READERS is a compelling reading programme for children. The programme is designed in conjunction with leading literacy experts, including Cliff Moon M.Ed., who has spent many years as a teacher and teacher educator specializing in reading. Cliff Moon has written more than 160 books for children and teachers. He is series editor to Collins Big Cat.

Beautiful illustrations and superb full-colour photographs combine with engaging, easy-to-read stories to offer a fresh approach to each subject in the series. Each DK READER is guaranteed to capture a child's interest while developing his or her reading skills, general knowledge, and love of reading.

The five levels of DK READERS are aimed at different reading abilities, enabling you to choose the books that are exactly right for your child:

Pre-level 1: Learning to read
Level 1: Beginning to read
Level 2: Beginning to read alone
Level 3: Reading alone
Level 4: Proficient readers

The "normal" age at which a child begins to read can be anywhere from three to eight years old. Adult participation through the lower levels is very helpful for providing encouragement, discussing storylines and sounding out unfamiliar words.

No matter which level you select, you can be sure that you are helping your child learn to read, then read to learn!

DK

LONDON, NEW YORK, MUNICH,
MELBOURNE, and DELHI

Project Editor Louise Pritchard
Art Editor Jill Plank

Senior Editor Linda Esposito
Senior Art Editor
Diane Thistlethwaite
Production Melanie Dowland
Picture Researcher Andrea Sadler
Illustrator Peter Dennis
Space Consultant Carole Stott
Indexer Lynn Bresler

Reading Consultant
Cliff Moon M.Ed.

Published in Great Britain by
Dorling Kindersley Limited
80 Strand, London WC2R ORL

Copyright © 2000 Dorling Kindersley Limited, London
A Penguin Company
This edition, 2013

2 4 6 8 10 9 7 5 3
002-187460 - 11/12

A CIP catalogue record for this book
is available from the British Library

ISBN: 978-1-40931-839-2

Colour reproduction by Colourscan, Singapore
Printed and bound in China by L Rex Printing Co., Ltd

The publisher would like to thank the following
for their kind permission to reproduce their photographs:
c=centre; b=bottom; l=left; r=right; t=top

Genesis Space Photo Library: 14cr; **N.A.S.A.:** 10cl; **Planet Earth
Pictures:** 4br, 15t, 30–31; **Popperfoto:** Reuters 12br; **Science Photo
Library:** A. Sokolov & A. Leonov/ASAP 20bl; **NASA:** 6, 11, 13, 21,
23, 26cl; **Times Syndication:** 7br.

All other images © Dorling Kindersley
For further information see: www.dkimages.com

Discover more at
www.dk.com

DK READERS

BEGINNING TO READ ALONE
2

Astronaut
Living in Space

Written by Kate Hayden

DK

A Dorling Kindersley Book

Linda is an astronaut
on the space shuttle.
She is going to repair
a broken telescope.
Linda loves going into space –
it is very exciting.
As she looks out of the window
she can see Earth far below.
What a view!
She can see towns and
rivers and mountains.

Telescopes

We can look at the stars
and planets through
telescopes on Earth.
But we can use telescopes
in space to see even further.

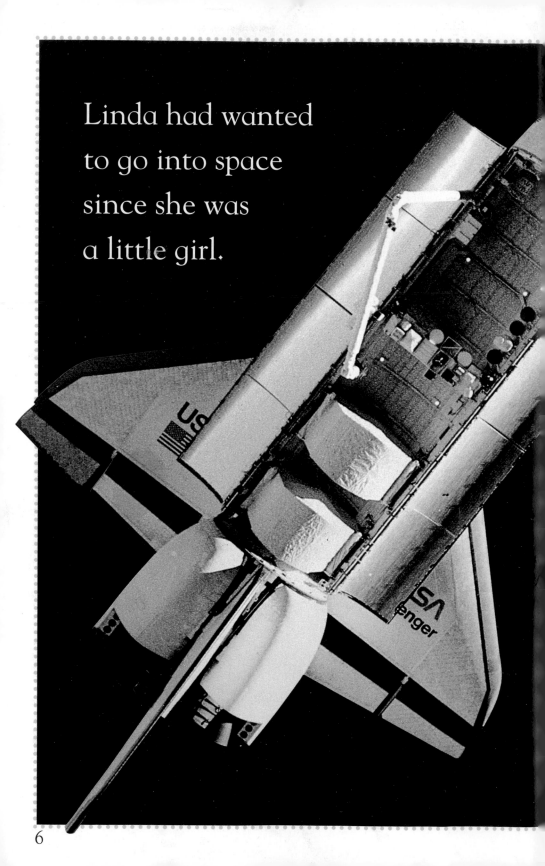

Linda had wanted
to go into space
since she was
a little girl.

When she applied for
a job as an astronaut,
thousands of other people
applied too.
But only six people
could get in.
Linda had to take lots of tests.
Doctors checked her heart,
lungs, eyes and ears.
Finally she got the job.
She was over the moon!

Science in space

Many astronauts are scientists.
Doctors study what happens
to our bodies in space.
Biologists study what happens
to plants and animals.

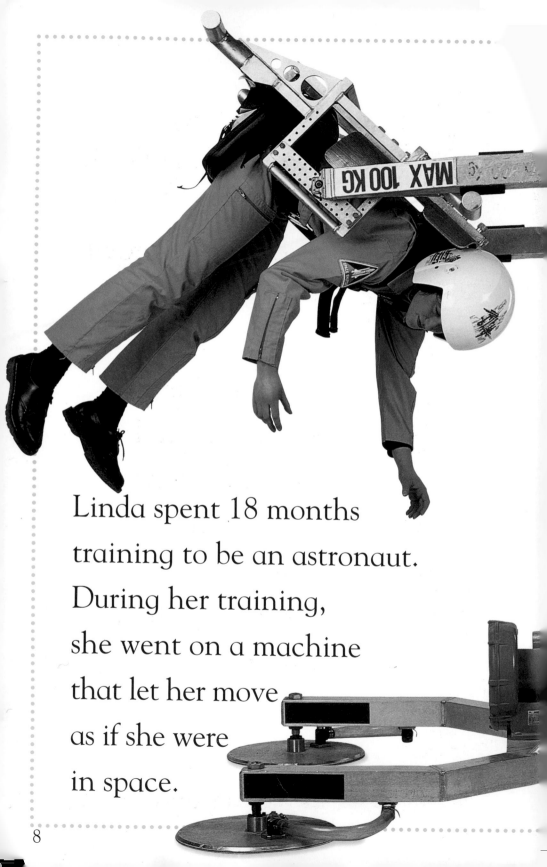

Linda spent 18 months
training to be an astronaut.
During her training,
she went on a machine
that let her move
as if she were
in space.

Space is very
different from Earth.
On Earth,
a force called gravity
keeps everyone
on the ground.
In space, there is
less gravity and
astronauts can
float around.
This is called
being weightless.
It happens
because of
the way the shuttle
moves around Earth.

Before each mission,
astronauts train for the job
they will do in space.
For this mission, Linda learned
how to repair a telescope.

 She practised
on a model
of a telescope
in a swimming pool –
being underwater
is a bit like

being in space.
Linda practised again and again
until she was perfect.
Then she was ready
to go up in the space shuttle.

This is Linda's fourth mission.
Each time the astronauts
strap themselves into their seats
Linda gets butterflies.
The final countdown begins.
Ten, nine, eight, seven, six, five,
four, three, two, one, lift-off!
There is a deafening, thundering
ROOAAARRRR
as the rockets fire the shuttle
off the launch pad.

Space suit
Astronauts wear
special orange suits
for take-off and landing.
The suits help them to cope
with the unusual forces.

People at Launch Control on Earth
watch the take-off.

They can talk to the crew
at any time.

In just 30 seconds,
the shuttle leaves
the blue sky
and enters
the darkness
of space.

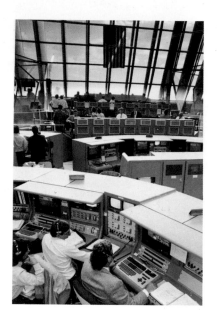

The rockets and fuel tank
drop away.

The rockets are collected
from the sea
to be used on
another mission.

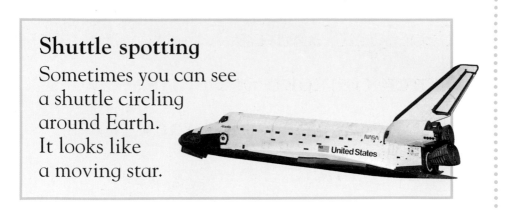

Shuttle spotting

Sometimes you can see
a shuttle circling
around Earth.
It looks like
a moving star.

Now Linda changes into trousers
and a T-shirt to relax.
She has pockets
for her pens and snacks
otherwise they will
float away.

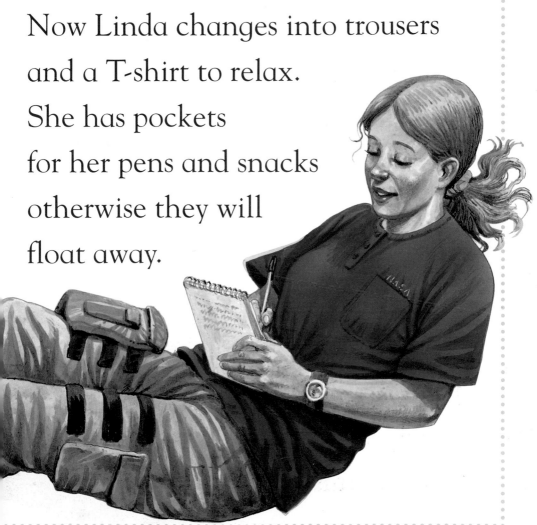

The space shuttle
is made up of three parts –
a space plane called the orbiter,
a fuel tank and two rockets.
The rockets fire the orbiter
into space.
The orbiter carries equipment,
such as a laboratory, or a telescope,
in the cargo bay.
The crew uses a robotic arm
to move things in and out of
the cargo bay.

There are eight astronauts
on Linda's mission.
They live and work in the cabin.
The mission commander,
who is in charge,
sits with the pilot
at the orbiter's controls.

A few hours after take-off,
some of the crew take a break and
Linda joins them for lunch.
She straps herself into a seat.
The food is in packages
held on a tray.
Linda ties her tray to her knee and
eats with a fork and spoon.
But she sucks her drink
out of a pack so the drops
don't float around.

Space food
There are more than
70 different kinds
of food available.
Some are ready-to-eat.
Others need water added.

Finally they reach
the broken telescope.
Linda puts on a special suit
for walking out in space.
It has oxygen for her to breathe
because there is no air in space.
It also has headphones and
a microphone in the helmet
so that Linda can talk to the crew.
A jet-propelled backpack
helps Linda move around.

Space walk
Russian astronaut
Alexei Leonov was
the first person
to walk in space,
in March 1965.

Out in space at last!
Linda begins to repair
the telescope.
But the telescope is bent and
her repair tool does not fit.
This means she must
get the telescope
into the cargo bay
to do the repairs.
Linda tells the commander
about her problem.
He moves out the robotic arm
to pick up the telescope.
But will it reach?
Linda stands on the arm
and gives directions.

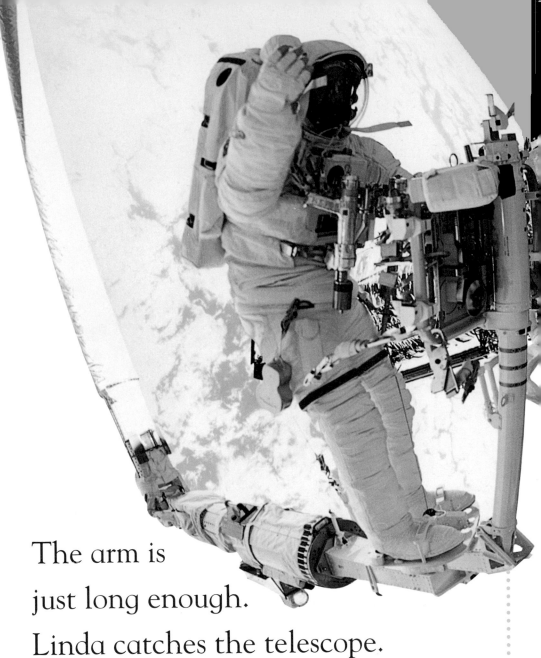

The arm is
just long enough.
Linda catches the telescope.
The commander brings it back
on the robotic arm
to the orbiter's cargo bay.

It takes a few hours
for Linda to repair the telescope.
Then she helps the commander
to put it back in space.
Linda is happy
that she has done her job.

Now Linda has to work out
on an exercise machine.
She is lighter in space
than on Earth,
so her bones and muscles
do not have to work very hard.
She must exercise
for two hours a day.
This stops her from growing weak.

Linda works hard on the machine. A doctor checks her health as she exercises.

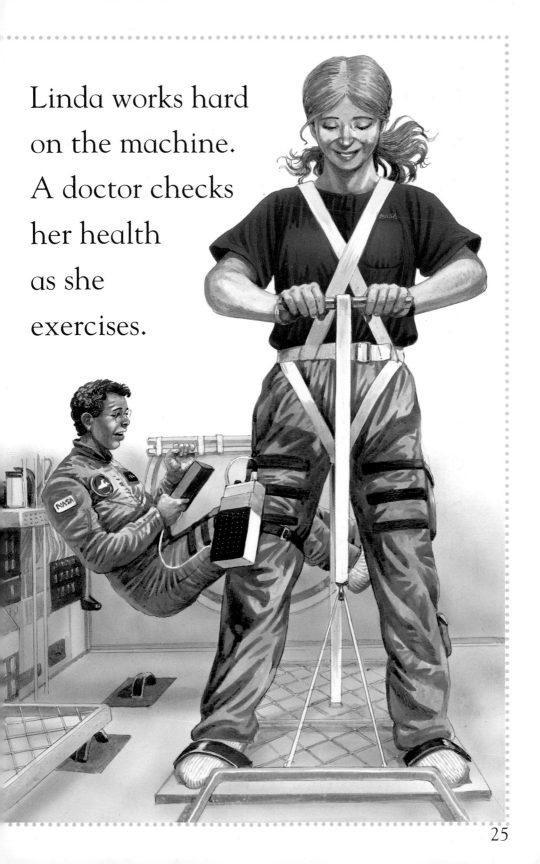

After her workout,
Linda washes with wet wipes.
There are no showers on board.
Drops of floating water
can damage the equipment.
There is a toilet though.

 It sucks everything
safely away.

Soon it is
Linda's turn to sleep.
She climbs into
a bunk on the wall and lies down.
The astronauts sleep in shifts,
so some of the crew
are always awake to work.

It is time to return to Earth!
It could be dangerous.
Earth is surrounded by
a blanket of gases
called the atmosphere.
The orbiter must re-enter
the atmosphere at
the perfect angle.
If it re-enters
too steeply, it will burn up.
If it comes down
at too shallow an angle,
it will bounce into space.
The pilot gets it just right.
The orbiter re-enters
the atmosphere safely.

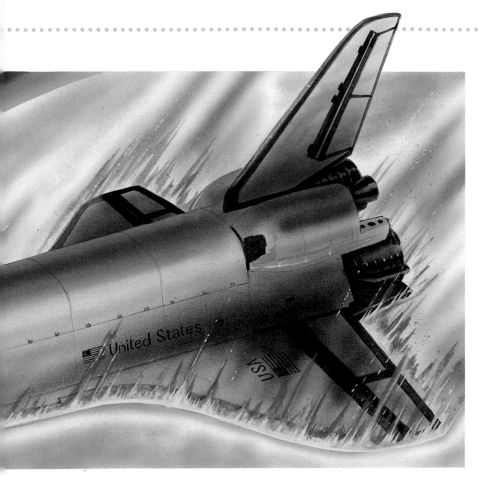

The orbiter is red-hot – it is 1,357°C (2,500°F), but it is covered with special tiles to stop it from burning up. Suddenly, Linda sees a tile fly past the window.

Linda does not worry.
There are still enough tiles
on the orbiter to protect it.
The orbiter starts to glide
through the air.

In only 14 seconds
the space craft will
touch down.
The pilot lowers
the landing gear.

Then the orbiter lands.
A drag chute, like a parachute,
helps to slow it down.
The astronauts have to wait for
the orbiter to cool down.
At last they come out.
Linda looks up into space.
She is already looking forward
        to her next mission.

Space facts

In space, astronauts are up to 19 millimetres taller than they are on Earth.

The heart does not need to pump as hard in space as it does on Earth, so it can get weak.

The astronauts in a space shuttle use up oxygen all the time, so fresh oxygen is circulated around the craft.

Water vapour from astronauts' breath is collected and recycled for drinking.

If an astronaut needs to shave, he must vacuum up the cuttings before they float away.

People in space can keep in touch with their family and friends using a laptop computer.

A woodpecker once delayed the launch of the space shuttle. It pecked more than 75 holes in the casing around the fuel tank.

The first creature to be born in space was a quail chick.